LISTENING TO Hindus

ROBERT JACKSON & ELEANOR NESBITT (Quakers)

Series Consultant: David Naylor
County General Adviser for Religious Education
in Hampshire

UNWIN HYMAN

Published in 1990 by
UNWIN HYMAN LIMITED
15/17 Broadwick Street
London W1V 1FP

British Library Cataloguing in Publication Data
Jackson, Robert, *1945–*
    Listening to Hindus.
    1. Hinduism
    I. Title   II. Nesbitt, Eleanor M.
    294.5

    ISBN 0–04–448121–7

Designed by Geoff Wadsley
Cover design by Ned Hoste/2H

Typeset by August Filmsetting, Haydock, St Helens
Printed and bound in Italy

Contents

Foreword

If you are going to benefit from using this book, you will need to follow some simple but important guidelines.

First, you must start with an open mind and really listen to the Hindus in this book. Second, be patient. The people you will be listening to are trying to express some difficult ideas. They will tell stories which have many layers of meaning and describe symbols which remind them of important truths. They may perform special acts and take part in ceremonies, some of which may be unfamiliar. Take time to listen to their explanations, to look below the surface and discover the meaning these activities and symbols have

for them. Third, remember that Hinduism is a world religion with millions of followers. You are only exploring a part of it and listening to some people's personal experiences. This book offers you a glimpse into the heart of their faith but always remember that there will be more to learn.

Finally, when you have finished listening and have thought about what you have heard, ask yourself the question, 'Is there anything which I can learn from this book about my own beliefs and values?'

David Naylor

A Journey into Hinduism

Some British Hindu children were asked to say what they thought was important about their way of life. Here are some of their answers.

'I don't eat meat.'
'You're not supposed to eat beef.'
'We have to speak the truth all the time.'
'Love your enemies and neighbours and don't make violence.'
'You pray every day.'
'Staying with the rules.'
'We perform a dance called garba.'
'You celebrate different things ... you celebrate Diwali if you're a Hindu.'

They were also asked what they'd miss most if they lived in a non-Hindu home. This is what some of the children said.

'I'd miss speaking my language.'
'The family, especially my gran. I'd miss the prayers and songs she'd be singing.'
'I'd miss going to the temple and all the gods.'
'I like the food in Indian religion.'
'I would miss praying.'

The variety of Hinduism

These answers give a taste of the Hindu tradition. Not all Hindus would agree with all the statements. Some Hindus do eat meat although they would be unlikely to eat beef as the cow is regarded as sacred, and not everyone believes in non-violence. Also there are great variations in language, festivals, music, dancing and cookery throughout India. Many of the gods are familiar to Hindus all over the country, but the names of some are known in only a few small areas.

Hinduism is a modern word, first used towards the beginning of the last century. It was used by Europeans to refer to the religious practices and beliefs of most of the people of India – those who were not Muslim, Christian, Buddhist or followers of any other religion. So, in some ways 'Hinduism' is a misleading word, for it refers to a multitude of people with a variety of beliefs and practices.

Some of the variations follow from the many differences in geography and culture in India. India is a huge country – over $2\frac{1}{2}$ million square kilometres – and it is composed of 18 states, many of which have their own languages and customs. The population is around 800 million, and about 80 per cent of these people are Hindu. Most live in villages, but about 20 per cent live in towns and huge cities such as New Delhi, Bombay, Calcutta and Madras. Other religious differences can result from individuals following the teachings of particular leaders, or from being especially devoted to a particular god or goddess. Some Hindus have left India and migrated to other parts of the world – to Canada, some African countries, and the United Kingdom, for example. There are now many young Hindus who were born in Britain and who keep up their families' religious traditions. This variety can be confusing but it is an accepted part of the Hindu tradition. In this book we will listen to a number of Hindus and learn something of what their religion means to them. Look for the big (❞) quotation marks which show you when you are **Listening to Hindus**.

Hinduism is full of contrasts. The large, modern temple opposite is in the capital of India, New Delhi. The little shrine below is in a small village in the state of Tamil Nadu in south India. You can see the contrasts between city and village and between a large, expensive building and a simple shrine built from local materials (the roof is made of leaves from the coconut palm). There are also contrasts of climate, culture, landscape and language between the north of India (where New Delhi is) and the south.

1 Think about your life at home, at school and in the community, and then make a list of things that you think are important in your way of life. Get into groups of four or five and compare your lists. Look for things in common and for differences and think of possible reasons for these. Report your findings to your teacher. See if there is anything in common between your list and the answers opposite.

The unity of Hinduism

❝Hinduism is a way of life, rather than a religion... The basis seems to be honesty, being unselfish, caring for others, and trying to bring about a betterment of mankind. If you can achieve that, then you are a good person. The whole aim of life should be to attain oneness with the Almighty; and if you can achieve that... then the Hindu philosophy says that you don't have to come back to this earth time and time again...❞

This personal description of Hinduism comes from Dr Gokal, a doctor at a hospital in Manchester. Some of the ideas which unite Hindus are mentioned by Dr Gokal. One is that Hinduism is a way of life, rather than a religion. Hinduism is very practical, and it includes rules of behaviour as well as all sorts of things that some people might think are nothing to do with religion. Your duties to members of your family, your attitude to your school work, what you eat for lunch or your family's choice of a date for a brother's or sister's wedding – to a Hindu all these are as much a part of their religious tradition as worshipping at home or going on a pilgrimage.

Dr Gokal also mentions the aim of achieving 'oneness with the Almighty'. Many Hindus believe that God is within each person. The trouble is that it is difficult for people to recognise this, and it may be necessary for a

The picture shows the life cycle of one person, from before birth until death.

soul to be born over and over again, over countless lifetimes, before that person realises the connection between the individual soul and God. The word for being reborn, as an animal or another person, is 'reincarnation'.

Moksha and yoga

Hindus believe that the purpose of life is to be reunited with God and so become freed from the cycle of rebirth into the world. This union with God and liberation from being reborn is often called 'moksha' or 'mukti'. Once moksha has been achieved a person's soul no longer returns to be reborn on earth. Most Hindus believe that moksha is possible if they surrender themselves to God. They do this through bhakti (loving devotion) to God. This devotion is usually expressed as worship in front of a picture or statue of God. People also repeat one of God's names, such as 'Rama' or 'Krishna', over and over again and they attend satsangs (gatherings). Everyone at the satsang sings hymns to God. There are two other ways of gaining moksha. One is through knowledge of the truth about God. The other is through doing the right deeds (karma). For Hindus this means worshipping with the correct rituals and carrying out all the duties expected of you at each stage in life, through childhood, youth, marriage, parenthood and so on.

Yoga means 'joining together' or union. It is the word used for these three ways of reuniting the human soul with God. The physical exercises which people also call yoga are meant to be a part of this 'training' of the soul to become closer to God. Certain exercises can help people to control their minds and relax their bodies so that they can concentrate more closely on God.

For most people bhakti (devotion) is the path which they can choose to bring them to God. No route to moksha is easy, and people can only achieve it if they serve God without thinking of getting any reward. At first many people need a reward, just like children who first enjoy going to the temple because they are given sweets there, but most people gradually progress beyond this reason for worship.

1 Look at the picture on p 6. With a group of friends write down what you think the message is meant to be for people who look at this display. Compare your answer with that of others in the class.

2 Discuss in a group ways in which you each seek liberation from everyday life and the world around you.

Gods and goddesses

In Hinduism there are many different gods and goddesses. Some of the main gods, such as Vishnu, Shiva and Brahma, and goddesses, for example Lakshmi, Saraswati and Santoshi Ma, are mentioned in this book. Different people choose different gods to worship, but they respect them all. Often, Hindus will say that since God is beyond our human understanding, each god or goddess gives us a clue to what God is like. God in the form of Ganesha – a rather plump young man with an elephant's head – shows, for example, that God can remove difficulties from people's lives in the same way as an elephant, by using its strong trunk, can remove obstacles from a road.

The idea of so many different gods and goddesses may seem complicated, but Hindu children learn their tradition in practical and straightforward ways – through living in a Hindu family, hearing stories, taking part in worship and festivals, being present at ceremonies such as weddings, and going on pilgrimages, which are special journeys to holy places.

3 With a group of friends, make a list of up to five things you would expect different religions to have in common. Explain your list to the rest of the class.

4 Using a tape recorder, with a group of friends make a short feature for a children's radio programme, explaining 'the unity and the variety of Hinduism'. There is no need to write everything out. Make notes to remind you of the points you want to make, for example, one God with many names, contrasts etc, and then take turns to speak using your own words. If you make a mistake, erase it and have another go. Play the tape to the rest of the class.

This picture of a marble image of Ganesha was taken at a Hindu temple in Coventry.

The Ganga at Varanasi

Certain places in India are regarded by many Hindus as being especially holy. Sometimes Hindus make pilgrimages to such places. Pilgrims travel for many different reasons – to give thanks, to ask for a blessing, to fulfil a vow. A vow is a solemn promise to God to perform a particular ceremony if a prayer is answered. A couple may pray for a child, for instance. If a baby is born, they may then fulfil their vow by travelling to a particular temple to offer thanks. Many want to feel the presence of God, by bathing in the waters of a sacred river or through seeing an image of a god or saint, believing that they receive God's blessing as their eyes meet the gaze of the image. Pilgrims hope that their acts of devotion will remove sin and help them gain merit.

Many holy places are on the banks of rivers. Ganga is the Indian name for a great river which flows down from the Himalaya mountains and across the plain of north India.

In English it is known as the Ganges. The river represents the goddess Mother Ganga. If you have ever felt the heat of India – often over 45°C in summer – and seen fields of crops dying from lack of water, you will understand why rivers are treated with so much love and respect.

When pilgrims reach the river bank they go down to the water's edge (there are special wide steps called ghats) and pray. They take a dip in the water or pour some over their heads. Many people fill a container with water. At home they will use this in daily worship. They give a little of this holy river water to any relative who is dying. Babu Govind Garala made the pilgrimage to the Ganga one year. He runs a post office in Coventry and is secretary of one of the local Hindu temples. Here is his description of the importance of the Ganga.

Pilgrims performing rituals and bathing in the Ganga at Varanasi (Benares) soon after sunrise.

Sunrise over the river Ganga at Varanasi (Benares). The sun is worshipped as Suryanarayan, the sun god.

❮Bathing in the Ganges has its special significance for Hindus. It is a sacred river and has always been called the mother goddess, Ganga. Many believe that bathing in the Ganga will take away your sorrows or your poverty and will help your progress on the religious path. It can be a religious turning point in your life. The water of Ganga is special. It is pure and will purify the whole human body. As the ancient myths put it, the Ganga falls from heaven and its function is to purify.

My personal view is that it is not the water which washes away sin. I think that being close to the holy men, the sannyasis, who follow their religious path by the river, encourages you to follow their example. In that way the Ganga removes your sins.❯

To bathe in the water of the Ganga as the sun comes up is an especially powerful experience, as Babu Govind Garala explains.

❮Dawn is a beginning, just like the beginning of our life. What better experience could a person have than dawn by the Ganga? The light is wonderful, and you can even stare at the sun. The atmosphere is tranquil and helps you to experience harmony. People offer prayers to mother Ganga and to the sun, Suryanarayan. They throw water from the Ganga towards Suryanarayan as an offering, reciting ancient prayers.❯

1 Read the passage where Babu Govind Garala talks about bathing in the Ganges. With a small group of friends list three reasons why many Hindus believe that bathing in this river is important.

2 With a small group of friends discuss Mr Garala's personal view about how the Ganges removes sins. Be ready to explain to the rest of the class what you think he means.

3 Find out about a pilgrimage made by either a Christian or a Muslim. Make a list of the reasons why the person went on the pilgrimage and compare them with the reasons given by Mina on p 10.

A pilgrimage in England

On these pages you can see pictures of Mina. She lives in Coventry. Religion is very important to Mina's family and she was one of 250 Hindus who took part in a pilgrimage to five temples, or mandirs, in England one day in 1987. Mina visited Hindu temples in Luton, Wellingborough, Woolwich and two in Leytonstone. In each temple she and the other pilgrims prayed in front of shrines, gave some money and received prashad. Prashad is food – usually fruit or Indian sweets – that has been offered to God. Here is her account of the journey.

❛It was a one-day journey to five different temples in England. Five is an auspicious number – a good one. In India you often have five places where you go. People who couldn't go to India decided to do the same here, so they chose five different types of mandirs – each one had something unique about it.

I like exploring. I'd been on a pilgrimage to India and everybody said it was going to be like that. I wanted to compare our mandir in Coventry with others and to see how people in other towns do what we do, here in Coventry. It was a good experience. I went for the religious reason too, to visit each temple and to pay my respects to God. The temple at Wellingborough – I enjoyed that most – made me feel as though we were in India. The arch shape and pillars reminded me of some of the mandirs in India.❜

---

1 Write a short piece of prose headed 'My favourite journey'. Like Mina, try to remember some different things which made the journey special.

2 Re-read Mina's words and find three reasons why she went on the pilgrimage.

Mina plays the tabla (drums) while everyone sings at a satsang – a meeting for worship – at her home in Coventry.

Mina describes what is happening in the picture (above) of the Wellingborough temple.

Mina with her older sister, Asha, in The Hindu Centre, Wellingborough.

❝The priest (we call him the pujari) is going round the shrines fanning them, as he would fan a king or queen. The women are paying their respects by bowing and offering money. When it was my turn I did the same as my sister – in the picture she's offering some money. Before I walked forward I folded my hands and closed my eyes.❞

3 Mina describes how worshippers use gestures (bowing, folding hands, closing eyes) and actions (fanning the images, offering money). Just as speech and writing are ways of communicating messages and ideas, so are gestures and actions. Re-read Mina's description and write down briefly what you think each gesture or action is 'saying'.

The Rathayatra

In London, every summer since 1968, hundreds of Hindus have joined in a Rathayatra. Rath (pronounced 'rut') is the word for a huge chariot and yatra means journey. Rathayatra is an annual chariot procession. On the chariot is a statue of Jagannath. Jagannath means Lord (nath) of the World (jagan). At the side of Jagannath there are images of his brother and sister. Rathayatra is always held on a Sunday in England. Whole families from Leicester, Coventry and other places come to enjoy a happy day out and to share in the blessing of Jagannath.

Hindus from many different groups join in the procession but it is especially important to members of the Hare Krishna movement. The Hare Krishna movement is also called the International Society for Krishna Consciousness (ISKCON). Members chant the words 'Hare Krishna'. These mean 'Krishna is Lord'. Most Hindus worship Krishna as one of the gods. They respect his teachings contained in the Bhagavad Gita, a holy book. But for members of ISKCON Krishna is the greatest god of all. Indeed, they believe that God *is* Krishna. There are members of ISKCON in many parts of the world. The organisation was founded by a Hindu called Prabhupada. He went to America in 1963, and later visited Britain. Most of the Hindus who join in the Rathayatra festival are not members of ISKCON. In fact, most Hindus are not members of religious organisations like this at all, although they may respect them, listen to their teachings and enjoy sharing in their festivals.

Ashish Anand is a Hindu boy who lives in Warwickshire. He and his family came to the Rathayatra by coach from a Hindu temple in Coventry. Ashish describes the festival.

❝Jagannath's Rathayatra changes dates, though it's usually in July. They have a big kind of rath, with an image of Jagannath.

The rath in this picture looks like the ones used in India but it can be taken to pieces so that it can be transported by lorry when necessary. The red and yellow dome can be raised or lowered to avoid catching on overhanging branches along the route. You can see the images of Jagannath and his brother and sister under the dome. There is a close-up of Jagannath on p 19.

Usually there are people pulling it, going right through the main roads of London. You'd be amazed by the number of people coming there, and they sing songs ... you have a nice day ... they put on plays about Krishna – and they give out chips and ice cream as well!❞

The act of pulling the rath is an important duty, says Subhash Anand, Ashish's father.

❝When you pull the rath with your hands, you are doing a devotional duty. You pull with your full force, you are absorbed mentally, and you receive God's blessing.❞

It was important to Ashish to take his turn at the ropes, as he explains.

❝People pull the rath as a way of bringing good luck and fortune to their family. That's why there are a lot of people pulling it. I pulled for about ten minutes and it was very enjoyable. The rath has three statues on it – Jagannath, his sister Subhadra and his brother Balarama. They do arti – that's making an offering of lighted lamps – all the way from Hyde Park to Battersea Park, and there are two people blowing conch shells. They give out prashad – food that's been offered to God – and flowers that have been offered as well. I enjoy the atmosphere of the Rathayatra most – all the people and the kirtan (that's the chanting) going on. 🍃

1 Receiving prashad is one way Hindus feel they receive God's blessing. Describe another way in which Subhash Anand felt he received God's blessing during the Rathayatra procession.

2 Make a list of things that you enjoy about a festival that you have celebrated – Christmas, for example, if you are from a Christian background. Now make a list of things that Ashish enjoyed about Rathayatra. Look for similarities and differences in the two lists.

Saral, Ashish's sister, adds

🍃 As the procession moves through the streets of London, other people join in, even if they are not Hindu. Some are a bit puzzled but they like watching, and others come and join in. It's enjoyable and it gives you peace of mind as well. 🍃

Devotees – including Subhash Anand and his daughter Saral – pulling the rath. it is decorated with fresh garlands of African marigolds, like the garlands frequently used in India. Saral explains, 'The rath is hand driven. Someone steers it but there's no engine; it's pulled by hand. I pulled for about half the journey. It was quite tiring at the beginning. The whole journey was about 5 km and took about 3 hours. You can see me near the end of the rope, wearing my pink check suit.'

For the Anands, like many Hindus, being vegetarian has a religious meaning. Subhash describes the meal they had at the Rathayatra.

The Anand family and some of their friends eating a vegetarian meal at the Rathayatra festival in London.

❦We were eating pure vegetarian food, which means it contains no meat, it's free from eggs and also from onions and garlic. We had vegetables, puri – that's a kind of bread – rice and some barfi – a sweet. We believe in vegetarianism: no meat, fish or eggs. The food we ate had been offered to the lord – it was prashad.❩

Many Hindus are strict vegetarians, using milk but avoiding any foods which contain animal fat or eggs. There are several reasons for this. Some may believe that the food they eat affects their character, so a person who eats meat, and even certain other foods such as onions, is less likely to be spiritual than someone who avoids these. Others also feel that you may be born again as an animal because you have caused its death. Even Hindus who do not follow these rules usually think that it is better to avoid meat, at least on some days of the year. They are least likely to eat beef, as cows are respected because they give us their milk. Ashish explains ISKCON's views on vegetarianism, by quoting from a Hindu holy book.

❝It says in the Bhagavad Gita, chapter 9, verse 26: 'If anyone offers to me, with love and devotion, a leaf, a flower, fruit or water I accept it'. It says nothing about eating meat. Members of ISKCON avoid all stimulants, whether it's alcohol or the caffeine in tea, coffee or coke. We drink water or fruit juice.❞

1 With a group of friends make a list of reasons for and against vegetarianism. Then make a list of reasons why many Hindus (such as those who belong to ISKCON) avoid eating meat. Using a cassette recorder, make a short feature for a children's radio programme called 'Is eating meat wrong?' You can have a

The Rathayatra festival at Puri in the state of Orissa, India.

presenter (who remains neutral) and contributors arguing different points of view. There is no need to write out a script – you can use your lists as 'prompts'. Play the tape to the rest of the class.

The biggest and most famous Rathayatra is at Puri, a town on the north-east coast of India. Hundreds of thousands of pilgrims visit Puri every year, and the most popular time to go there is for the Rathayatra. Over a hundred years ago, British visitors to the festival thought that the name Jagannath referred to the chariot rather than the god. This is how the word juggernaut came into the English language, as a word meaning a huge lorry.

2 Which of these words do you think come from one of the Indian languages? Look them up in a dictionary to check if you are right: bungalow; maisonette; blouse; pyjamas; jodphurs; khaki; orange; pickle; chutney; perfume; shampoo; verandah; balcony.

Stories

Mina and Ashish enjoy listening to and retelling Hindu stories. Sometimes they hear them from relatives or in the temple. They read books of stories too. In one popular series the stories are printed as comics. At festival times ancient stories are sometimes acted out as plays and occasionally the children take part. They particularly like watching videos of Hindu stories, when the giants, gods and demons really come to life. One famous story tells how the river Ganga came down to earth through the efforts of Bhagirath, the great-great-grandson of King Sagara. Here is part of the story.

The Ganga comes down to earth

King Sagara had 60,001 sons. The gods felt that the King and his sons were too full of earthly pride. Eventually, the god Vishnu punished them for their proud and difficult behaviour and burned King Sagara's sons to ashes. When Sagara's grandson discovered what had happened, a wise man informed him that his uncles would only come back to life if the holy river Ganga flowed over their ashes.

King Sagara, who reigned for 30,000 years, tried and tried but could not persuade the mother goddess Ganga to come down from heaven and restore his sons. His grandson and great-grandson also failed. But the next king, Bhagirath, his great-great-grandson, prayed and fasted so much that Lord Brahma at last agreed to command Ganga to descend to earth.

If, however, the waters of the Ganga had all fallen at once, everything on earth would have been swept away and destroyed. So Bhagirath continued praying and fasting until Lord Shiva agreed to catch the torrent of water in his hair, so dividing Ganga into seven different streams. One of these became the earthly River Ganga and its pure waters flowed over the ashes of King Sagara's many sons. In this way Sagara's sons were purified by the Ganga and their souls at last rose to heaven.

Look carefully at the picture below showing part of a huge carving on a rock face at

By his carvings on this rock face, over a thousand years ago, a sculptor told the story of the Ganga coming down to earth.

This popular picture shows the Ganga flowing from the hair of Lord Shiva. Shiva is a god who is worshipped by many Hindus. He has other names, too, such as Mahesh, Mahadeva, Shankara. Sometimes he is called 'the destroyer' because his power destroys the world before it is again created. But, as the story about the Ganga reveals, he also prevents destruction. This picture shows him as a holy man living a simple life, performing yoga and meditating. He has a weapon called a trident, his hair is piled high, he wears a necklace of cobras and his body is smeared with ashes. In the background you can see the Ganga flowing from the Himalaya mountains, and on its banks a white bull is resting. This is Nandi, the bull on which Shiva rides. Many Hindu gods have an animal associated with them. Ganesha has a rat, and the goddess Durga has a lion.

Mahabalipuram in south India. It is about 7 metres high and 25 metres long, and has over 100 figures of gods, people and animals. For a long time people thought the carvings told the story of a character called Arjuna. Now most people agree that it shows the moment when the Ganga flowed onto the earth. See if you can find the river bed. Can you see the King and Queen of the nagas (snakes) swimming up the falling river? Can you find the figure of Bhagirath, standing on one leg and holding a stone above his head as part of his prayers to ask Brahma to command the river to descend to earth? Notice that the elephants and the figures nearest the river are looking inwards to see the miraculous descent of the river. Below the elephant's tusk you can see a cat holding its paws above its head, imitating Bhagirath!

1 Draw the story of the Descent of the Ganga as a comic strip. Now cut out your pictures so they are all separate, and shuffle them together like a pack of cards. Then ask a partner to arrange them in the right order and re-tell the story to you.

2 Stories often help us to understand the world by explaining, for example, some of the mysteries of nature. Make a list of some reasons why you think the story of the Ganga was first told. Explain these to your partner.

17

Here is a story which helps us to understand why Jagannath, 'Lord of the Universe', appears as he does in images and pictures. It reminds Hindus that their search for God may take a long time, and that no image can ever really show what God is like. Saral was told this story by her uncle on the coach going to Rathayatra, as a way of explaining the meaning behind the festival.

The image of Jagannath

There was once a King who longed to serve God. One day a pilgrim arrived and told him that he had seen God, on a distant mountain top. The King sent his chief priest to find this special place. When at last the priest reached the mountainous area described by the pilgrim, he stayed and began to share the life of the poor people he found there, who herded pigs and worshipped God. Eventually he managed to persuade their leader to reveal God to him, but only on the condition that he agreed to be led blindfold to the special place. The priest accepted but he had a clever idea – he sprinkled mustard seeds all along the path, knowing that when these sprouted they would mark out the route. Then the King would also be able to find the way to God.

The priest returned to the King, told him what had happened and brought him to the mountain top, where he in turn followed the trail of mustard plants. But when the King arrived at the special place – God had disappeared. The King was told that God would reappear only when a huge temple had been built. The King ordered this to be done, and then he learned that Jagannath, Lord of the Universe, would appear in the form of a piece of wood. He waited and waited – but nothing happened. Many more years passed and the King remained just as determined to see God. One night he had a dream, which revealed a place by the sea where he would find an enormous tree trunk floating on the waves.

He set off straightaway to find the tree trunk and asked his bodyguards to lift it out of the water, but it was far too heavy for them. Even strong elephants couldn't move it. Just then a holy man – a swami – appeared and lifted the log from the water all by himself. It was taken to a room to be carved into a statue, but the King's sculptors could make no impression on the hard wood, however much they tried. Again the swami appeared, saying he could carve the image as long as no one watched. The King promised that no one would look, so the swami was locked alone in the room with the tree trunk. For five days and nights he carved the wood, not even stopping to eat or sleep. But by the sixth day the King was so impatient that he broke his promise and opened the door. The swami had disappeared, leaving behind an image of Jagannath – but one without hands or feet.

The King was sad and blamed his own impatience, until one day he heard that written in an ancient holy book were the words 'God has no hands or feet'. Even without these, realised the King, God blesses us and accepts what we have to offer.

---

1 Make up your own version of the story of Jagannath. You may be able to record it on a cassette recorder. Play the tape to a younger child, perhaps a brother or sister.

2 Stories are often meant to make us think or to teach us lessons. We have already mentioned some of the lessons that can be learned from the story of Jagannath. Write down anything else which you think the story tells us. Discuss your ideas with a partner.

The image of Jagannath at the Rathayatra festival in London, 1988.

Stories and festivals

If Saral had not gone to Rathayatra she might not have been told the story about Jagannath. Many stories are connected with particular festivals. Each year, when a festival comes round, children hear the stories connected with it from their parents and other adults. Hindu children who attend classes to learn an Indian language or to find out more about their religion often rehearse dances or dramas which tell a particular story. Sometimes they perform these in the temple or in a hall which has been specially hired for the festival celebrations.

Many festivals have been celebrated for hundreds of years. There are usually several stories about how they began and why they are celebrated. Children may hear different stories, depending on which part of India their family comes from. For instance, at the autumn festival of Diwali many Hindus remember the story of King Rama and Queen Sita returning to their kingdom after fourteen years in exile.

But in different areas of India other stories are told. Some of these are about Lakshmi, the goddess of wealth and prosperity. There are also a variety of stories connected with the spring festival of Holi. It is celebrated in a number of different ways, but for families from Gujarat (and most British Hindus are Gujaratis) the festivities usually include a bonfire. Holi is a wonderful excuse for people

In this picture you can see the image of Jagannath (right) with images of his brother, Balarama, and his sister, Subhadra. A woman is garlanding the image of Jagannath. French and African marigold flowers threaded together are often made into garlands in India. Putting a garland on a statue or picture shows respect for the god or goddess which it represents. For the same reason, Hindus often garland honoured guests and a bride and bridegroom garland each other.

Above: Here you can see a young man carving a wooden statue. He is learning how to be a sculptor at a college in Mahabalipuram, south India. Religious statues are also made from stone and metal. Marble is very popular.

Below: For Gujarati children in Britain the bonfire is usually the most exciting part of the Holi festival. British weather at this time is often cold and wet, and it can be difficult to throw coloured water and powders everywhere. Everyone enjoys sharing coconuts and popcorn roasted in the fire.

to let off steam. Everyone usually gets drenched with coloured water and covered in coloured powder! One story told at Holi is about Prince Prahlada refusing to worship his evil father, King Hiranyakashipu. In this story Hiranyakashipu's wicked sister, Holika, tries to kill Prahlada by burning him but he is protected by the power of Vishnu, while she herself is burned to death.

Chetan, a ten-year-old Gujarati boy who has celebrated Holi in Coventry many times, knows of another story about Holi which explains why Hindus throw coloured water and powder at each other. His mother had told him that when Lord Krishna was small he used to throw cream or milk over the milkmaids. He thought it was such fun that he threw colours on them! Another story which links Krishna with Holi explains why some Gujarati parents carry their babies around the bonfire, as a way of expressing their wish to protect them from harm. This tradition is a reminder of a story about a demon who tried to kill Krishna when he was a baby by giving him poisonous milk from her breast. He did not die, as other babies had done, because of his divine power. Instead, the demon shrivelled up and died, leaving Krishna completely unharmed. There is more about this early part of Krishna's life in the caption on p 44.

1 Here are some questions to discuss with a partner or in a small group. Do you think these stories really happened? Does a story have to be about a real event for it to teach us something? Can you think of any fictional television programmes or films that tell stories which have a lesson or message for us? Think of three examples which you could talk about to the rest of the class.

When Ashish's little brother Amit is naughty his family call him 'mahkhan chor'. This means 'butter thief'. It is an affectionate nickname for Lord Krishna, who got up to all sorts of mischief as a human child. Many Hindus believe that Krishna was really the god Vishnu in human form, who had been born on earth to help the human race.

Krishna, the naughty child

As a child, Krishna was brought up by his loving foster parents, Nanda and Yashoda. He enjoyed playing with the other village children. They often played among the cattle and Krishna sometimes mischievously untied the calves, which then ran all over the place.

Every day the village women milked the cows and made fresh yoghurt. Out of this they made butter by churning the yoghurt in a big round pot. Sometimes Krishna stole milk, yoghurt and butter from the pots in which these were kept.

This meant climbing up on a pile of pillows to reach them as they were hung from the roof. Sometimes he dropped and broke the pots but, after one look at his beautiful face, Yashoda always forgave him!

One day the other children told her that Krishna had been eating dirt from the ground. Yashoda was cross with him but Krishna protested, 'I haven't eaten any dirt. If you don't believe me, look inside my mouth'. Yashoda did so. As Krishna opened his mouth she saw to her amazement not dirt but the whole universe. She saw the sky and the earth, the wind and the lightning, the moon and the stars. At once her anger vanished, and she felt even more love for her wonderful son.

This picture shows the god Krishna with his brother Balarama. They are stealing from their mother's butter pot.

This picture shows Lord Krishna (right) with Prince Arjuna and his chariot on the battlefield. The Prince is unhappy because he has been forced into battle against his own relations. Krishna encourages him in his duty, saying that sometimes it is right to do what seems most difficult. His words to Arjuna can be read in the Bhagavad Gita, the 'Song of the Lord'. For many Hindus this is their most holy book, which guides them through life.

1 In a group, divide the story into a series of events. Each person in the group can then illustrate one of the events with a painting or collage. When all the pictures are finished they can be displayed in the correct order.

2 With help from your teacher, take colour slides of your group's pictures. These can be shown to younger children while you tell your own version of the story. Pause before you change each slide and see if the children can guess what happens next.

3 Stories about how God's love or power can be experienced through ordinary people are to be found in many of the world's religions. Make up a story of your own on this theme.

In the Hindu tradition there are many stories about Krishna, often as a child. Others show him as a teenager, a handsome cowherd who plays the flute and with whom the gopis (milkmaids) fall in love. Then there is Krishna the hero, a brave warrior who fights great battles. In a book called the Bhagavad Gita (the Song of God), Krishna is shown as God who has come to earth in human form to help put things right when people have not been living good dutiful lives. In the picture you can see him talking to prince Arjuna. Devotees of Krishna sometimes say that these stories show the strength of God's love for people. Sometimes this is pictured as the love between a child and mother, or between two people in love with each other, or between friends with complete trust in one another. On the next page you can read another famous story about Krishna and you can see a picture of him with his favourite gopi, Radha, on p 44.

Learning with Hindu friends

Like a growing number of Hindu children in Britain, Mina regularly attends classes where she learns more about her religion. The classes she goes to are attended by followers of a famous guru, or religious teacher, who lives in south India. He is called Sathya Sai Baba. These classes are called Bal Vikas (meaning 'child development'). The children look forward to meeting their friends from other schools, singing bhajans (devotional songs) together and hearing stories about the gods and great people. They learn new prayers and bhajans, and discuss their ideas about right and wrong.

Every year many of the children attend a youth camp. Here is a story which Mina saw performed by puppets at a youth camp held in Coventry. It shows the great love which a princess called Meera felt for Krishna. The songs which she sang are still very popular.

Princess Meera

About 500 years ago Princess Meera was born to a royal family in the city of Chitor, in a part of India famous for the bravery of its kings.

One day, when she was five years old, the princess stood on the palace balcony watching a bridegroom ride past the palace to his wedding. He was covered with flowers and wore splendid clothes. He was followed by a joyful procession. In her excitement Meera asked, 'Where is my bridegroom?' Her mother pointed to a statue of Krishna and said, 'Krishna is your bridegroom.' Meera became fascinated by the statue. She began to talk to Krishna, and would dance and sing in front of him.

Left: Here are the children at the Bal Vikas summer camp. This lasted for a weekend and was held in a church hall in Coventry in 1986. The children are dressed in white because this colour represents purity. At the camp there are games and competitions, and the children take part in music and dance.

Right: The picture of Meera is from a calendar. In the picture you should be able to find lots of examples of a Hindu symbol that looks rather like a number 3 – see how many you can find. In Sanskrit letters this spells 'om' or 'aum' (it rhymes with 'dome'). Turn to p 39 to read more about this symbol.

While she was still very young Meera was married to a prince, but she still thought of Krishna as her real husband and refused to worship in front of any other images of God. This annoyed her husband's family. Meera spent most of her time dancing and singing for Krishna, and news of the 'strange princess' spread far and wide.

After Meera's husband had died in battle his brother became King. Several times he tried to kill Meera, because she refused to do what he wished, but he always failed. When he sent a cup of poison for her to drink, it turned into nectar thanks to Krishna's power. A deadly cobra which he sent her in a basket turned into a harmless garland of flowers which she put round her neck.

As the King was treating her more and more cruelly, Meera decided to leave Chitor. She headed north to Vrindaban, the place where Krishna had lived on earth as a young man. The King tried to fetch her back but she went to Krishna's temple and danced in joy before his statue. As she danced, Meera and Krishna became one and the same. Now she could never be separated from Krishna. She was completely one with God.

1 Look at the picture of Meera. Write a paragraph telling in your own words the part of the story that the picture illustrates. If you want more information about Krishna before you write, turn back to pp 22 and 23.

Worship

The home shrine

Most Hindu families have a place of worship in their house. A whole room may be used as a shrine. The first picture shows a woman doing puja – performing worship – in the shrine room at the house of a wealthy family in the south Indian city of Madras. Usually shrines are smaller than this and may simply consist of a group of religious pictures on a shelf. Besides pictures of gods and goddesses there will be incense sticks and other things which Hindus use when they pray. These help them to concentrate their thoughts on God. You can see some of these in the picture showing Mrs Soni praying at the shrine at her home in Bombay, a large city on the north-west coast of India.

Hindus wash thoroughly before praying at the shrine. They never go up to it with their shoes on. By removing their footwear, they keep the area around the shrine cleaner and show their respect.

Different families will have pictures of different gods and, even within the same family, some members may pray more to one particular god or goddess. Many Hindus would explain this by saying that God is really one and that these different gods and goddesses are like different photographs of a person whom we love and that – like a photograph – none of them is the actual person, just a representation of him or her.

Many Hindus try to pray every day. This means that they focus their thoughts on God. They may simply light an incense stick and wave it in a clockwise, circular motion in front of the picture of a god or goddess. They may sit cross-legged on the floor in front of the shrine, reading from a religious book or repeating special words with the help of a 'mala'. The mala looks like a necklace and has 108 beads. People find it is easier to concentrate if they hold each bead in turn as they repeat the words. Words repeated in prayer are called a 'mantra'. A mantra may consist of one word or several. By repeating them people believe that they are releasing their spiritual power. For example, one mantra is 'om shanti', a prayer for peace. When people repeat this they believe that they and the world around them will become more peaceful.

In many households it is the older people, the grandparents, who spend most time praying. Hindus feel it is right that younger members of the family should be occupied mainly in earning a living and bringing up their children. It is usual to devote more time to praying later in life.

A shrine in a house in Madras, south India.

1 With a group of friends list as many words as you can think of connected with the word 'worship'. Now divide them into groups of words that you think go together. Think of a heading for each group of words. Do a flow diagram with the word 'worship' in the middle and your headings around it. Compare your diagram with others from your class and discuss the differences.

Mrs Pushpa Soni, many members of whose family live in Britain, worships at the shrine in her flat in Bombay, India. She has lit the arti lamp.

27

A priest visits a home

Two stages in a puja at the Anands' house led by a brahmin priest.

Hindu families belong to castes. In the past, members of one caste would all follow the same occupation. In the goldsmith caste nearly everyone made jewellery. Members of the tailor caste would all make and sell clothes. Once born into a caste a person is a member of it for life and normally marries someone from the same caste. The occupation of men from the brahmin castes was to read holy books and look after places of worship. Nowadays most brahmins earn a living in other ways but some still carry out religious duties. The brahmin priest tells the family what they must say and do as part of the puja. Puja means the worship of God with prayers, offerings of fruit, flowers and so on. Sometimes a priest is invited to the house to conduct a puja.

Yashpal Joshi is a brahmin who works as a priest in Coventry. These pictures show him performing and explaining to the Anand family the main stages in the puja. Before taking part in the puja everyone must first wash thoroughly. As the family sit on the floor near the priest he tells them each to drink a little water which contains drops of Ganga river water. They have already made themselves outwardly clean. By drinking this special water they believe they will become inwardly pure too.

In the first picture of the puja Yashpal Joshi is putting a tilak – a red mark – on Subhash Anand's forehead. This is a sign that the puja is beginning. He has also placed flowers on his head. Everyone then worships Ganesha.

28

Ganesha is the god who has an elephant's head and, like a strong elephant, can remove obstacles and difficulties. People often pray to Ganesha at the beginning of ceremonies and special occasions. God is treated like a guest who is being welcomed and is offered sweets, sultanas and almonds. Later everyone will eat these as prashad (holy food). You can see the book from which the priest reads, the thread which he has tied on to Subhash Anand's right wrist as one of the first stages in worship, and some more lengths of red thread to be used later in the puja.

The second picture shows a later stage in the puja. You can just see the flame of a lamp in the bottom left-hand corner. On the tray there is a leaf with a betel nut resting on it, as well as some flower petals. There are stainless steel vessels containing coloured powders and a beaker of water. Ashish's parents follow the priest's instructions, and the children join in when asked to. The priest must make sure that the puja is performed correctly, so everyone concentrates on his directions. Instructions for the words and actions of the ritual are laid down in ancient books, but they are also passed on by word of mouth by brahmins from generation to generation.

Performing ritual actions is important for Hindus. But Hindu worship can also include meditation, when people stay quite still, calming the body and the mind together in order to concentrate on God.

---

1 Many religions have priests. With the help of your teacher find out some similarities and some differences between the work of Hindu priests and priests from a Christian denomination.

Mina's cousin, Krishna, performing arti in front of a picture of Sathya Sai Baba in their house. Sai Baba wears a red robe. The picture frame has been covered with red cloth as a sign of respect.

Satsang

Many Hindus are inspired by a guru, who is a religious teacher. Some believe that their guru is God in human form. Mina is one of thousands of Hindus and others who follow Sathya Sai Baba, a guru who lives in Puttaparthi in south India. With her family she travelled all the way from Coventry to see him there and to share in his sixtieth birthday celebrations. She refers to him as Swami (lord) or as Baba. People feel that they receive God's blessing simply by seeing and being in the presence of such a spiritual person. They call this experience or glimpse of God 'darshan'. Here is Mina's description of her journey.

❝We arrived at 5.30 in the morning at Bombay. At 6 o'clock we left for Bangalore. From there, we went in a car and a van to Puttaparthi. Every day we travelled there and back, to receive Swami's blessing. We sat in line for his darshan. Swami had a canteen built for foreigners. Everything was clean. There was free food for ten days for fifteen thousand people. On his birthday sixty helicopters, with big lights like stars, came from the mountains. At the end he was swinging on a silver swing.❞

In Mina's house in Coventry there is a shrine upstairs where all the family worship each day. One end of the living room is also set out as a shrine. Each evening Mina and her family pray and sing bhajans, or religious songs, here. On at least one evening a week they are joined by other families. Mina often leads the singing – in four different languages: English, Gujarati, Hindi and Sanskrit. Sometimes she plays the harmonium. This has a keyboard which she plays with her right hand, while pumping air in and out with her left. In the picture on p 10 she is playing the tabla, a pair of drums which are specially tuned and played with the fingers and palms of both hands. After the songs a special prayer, called 'arti', is always sung. Mina describes the arti ceremony which takes place at her home.

❝First we light a metal lamp. In our house we use a lamp with one or five cotton wicks soaked in ghi – that's melted butter. If you have five flames it represents our five senses, and if you have just one flame it is to say 'God and I are as one'.

You take the lamp in your right hand and turn it in a circle clockwise in front of Baba's picture. When you get to the bottom of the circle, you move it from left to right to left and then up again to complete the circle. Later the flames are offered: you hold the arti lamp in your left hand and direct the flames with your right, first towards Baba's picture, then towards everyone. In the mandir people would be given things like nuts and fruit as prashad. We give out vibhuti – it's a kind of powder with a sweet taste. It comes from Prasanthi Nilayam, Baba's headquarters in India.

When I perform arti I think of it as giving my mind peace and rest, instead of always asking 'God give me this' or 'God give me that'. If I do it at the end of the day I say 'Thank you God, for such a good day'. I don't perform 'vrats' (promising to do something like keeping a fast) because I think that means you're always asking God for something. I think he's given you enough – food, clothing and so on.❞

The arti ceremony for followers of Sathya Sai Baba is very similar to arti as it would be performed in many Hindu temples. There are some differences: the lamp is directed towards a picture of Sathya Sai Baba rather than a traditional picture or image of a god or goddess, some of the prayers are different, and vibhuti is distributed at Sathya Sai Baba's arti. Vibhuti is a fragrant powdery ash that has Sathya Sai Baba's blessing.

Many people attend the satsangs at Mina's house. Mina's family are dedicated followers of Sathya Sai Baba, but those who attend the satsang need not be members of his organisation, though they respect him and listen to his teaching.

Mina distributes vibhuti, after the arti ceremony.

1 What is a guru? Why do some Hindus have gurus and what do they gain from them? Would you like to have a guru? Give reasons for and against.

2 Make a list of the stages in the arti ceremony from lighting the lamp to the distribution of prashad and vibhuti. Discuss what you think is the meaning of each stage with your partner and report back to the rest of the class.

3 For Mina, arti has an 'inward' as well as an 'outward' side. Read what Mina says about her thoughts and prayers during arti. Choose a phrase from Mina's words that would make a good headline for the whole paragraph.

Fasting

Hindu women often keep fasts. Usually this does not mean going without food and drink completely. There are different rules for different kinds of fast. Some are kept on a particular day of the week for a certain number of weeks. Some fasts come once a year. Usually women fast, beause they believe this will somehow bring God's blessing on their husbands and children. When the fast is over they serve a special meal.

Some women fast for a certain number of Fridays in succession, in the hope that Santoshi Ma (the goddess of contentment) will bless their families. Each Friday they read the story of Santoshi Ma, which has now been made into a popular film. On the last Friday of their fast, they invite eight boys for a meal. Each boy gets a present. It is a rule that on this day nothing sour or bitter can be eaten.

Santoshi Ma

A story connected with this tradition tells of a time when Santoshi Ma helped an unhappy woman. The woman's husband had gone away from home, leaving her alone with her mother-in-law and sisters-in-law, who were unkind to her. They sent her to the forest each day to collect firewood and only gave her water to drink and a coarse kind of bread. One day she met some women who told her that Santoshi Ma would bring her happiness, provided she followed the rules for keeping the fast properly. These rules included giving a meal to her sisters-in-law's sons but making sure they did not eat anything at all sour, such as citrus fruit and tomatoes.

Soon after this she began to fast every Friday, carefully following the instructions she had been given. Santoshi Ma then appeared to the woman's husband in a dream and told him to return home. Straight away he sent his wife a letter and some money and started on his journey home. The woman brightened up at the good news but her eldest sister-in-law, hating to see her so happy, told her sons to eat something sour after the sweet food which their aunt served them. By doing this, they broke the rules of the fast and displeased the goddess. In her anger, Santoshi Ma caused the woman's husband to be arrested. The poor woman then made sure that no one ate the sour food again on the day of her fast. Santoshi Ma, now pleased, came to the house in disguise to frighten the unkind in-laws and to bless the woman who had suffered so much. Her husband returned home and, to their joy, they later had a child.

---

1 Have you ever gone without food for a complete day, perhaps for a sponsored fast to raise money for famine victims, or for some other reason? Write a short report of why you fasted and what it felt like. Then explore the idea of 'going without' in more general terms – giving up something, not just food, as a means of achieving something else.

2 Not all Hindus share the same views about fasting. Look again at what Mina says about fasting on p 31 and write down her reasons for not fasting.

Right: **These two girls are goynis. Hema stands in front of her aunt who pours a little water over her big toe and then decorates the nail with red powder and rice grains. After this she puts a red mark on Hema's forehead and gives her some money and a sweet. The family are making a video of the ceremony and can watch what is happening on the TV screen which you can see in the background.**

Mina, like many Hindus in Britain, is Gujarati. This means that her ancestors come from part of India called Gujarat. They speak Gujarati and eat Gujarati food. (You can see what Gujarati writing looks like on the invitation card on p 60). Many Gujarati Hindu girls have the chance to be 'goynis' on certain occasions. Goynis are living symbols of the goddess (Devi) and are treated with great respect. They can be either young girls – usually twelve or less – or married women. They are invited to share a meal at the house of a woman who has been keeping a fast that day. As well as food, she gives them bangles, sweets or other small gifts.

Goddesses

Since, for many Hindus, God is everywhere and is present in everything, it is not surprising that God is often pictured in female as well as male form. Santoshi Ma is just one of the countless forms of Devi, the goddess, who represents different aspects of God's power. Ma, Mata and Mataji all mean 'mother' and are all used as titles for Devi. Saraswati is the goddess of education and the arts and is likely to be worshipped by schoolchildren and students. Lakshmi is the goddess of wealth and prosperity. She is especially worshipped at the festival of Diwali. Some goddesses, like Durga, who rides on a lion and slays a demon in the form of a buffalo, are fierce and terrifying. On pages 48 and 49 you can read about the installation of an image of a goddess at a temple in Coventry.

Left: **Santoshi Ma. Her name means 'Mother (goddess) of contentment'. People only began to worship her about 30 years ago. Many began to do so after seeing the film about her. In the picture you can see the boys who have been invited to receive food when the fast is over and the women who worship the goddess.**

3 Look carefully at the picture of Santoshi Ma. Can you see: a group of boys being given a meal containing nothing sour; the wife who faithfully kept the fast; the husband returning home; and a priest beside a sacred fire? Look for clues which suggest that Santoshi Ma has a kind side to her character and a stern side that can deal out punishment. Why do you think the artist shows Santoshi Ma with four arms?

4 With a group of friends make a list of Ganesha's qualities (see p 7) and another one of Santoshi Ma's qualities. Report back to your teacher the similarities and differences between the two.

Gods and goddesses are sometimes linked with one another in Hindu stories and pictures, and share certain qualities. Sometimes this is done by relating them together in families. The picture shows that Santoshi Ma is connected with Shiva: she holds a trident, a weapon associated with Shiva (see the picture of Shiva on p 17). The four arms represent the goddess's power, and hold several symbols of these powers. Her lower right hand is raised in blessing in a gesture which means 'Do not fear'. Her lower left hand holds a bowl of sweet rice pudding which she has accepted as an offering. The weapons show her stern side.

33

Worship in the temple

In most temples there is a brahmin who is employed to lead daily worship and to look after the shrine. Every day he offers food in front of the images of the gods and he gives prashad to the worshippers who visit the temple.

People may come to the temple at any time. In the early morning and evening they join in the arti ceremony. Ashish and his family usually go on Tuesday evenings. Sometimes people gather together to read a holy book such as the Ramayana. This tells the story of the good King Rama, his devoted brother and his faithful wife. People enjoy listening to their adventures and learning from them how people should behave to one another.

In this picture a couple are performing a puja. They have holy water in their hands. The priest (right) tells them what to do while other people watch. They are sitting in a temple in Coventry, which used to be a school building and was converted into a place for worship by the local Hindu community. Notice the various things which are being offered in worship, including flower petals and fruit. The coconut placed on a bed of leaves on a copper water vessel is a symbol of the goddess.

In Britain, unlike in India, most temples are in buildings which were first used as houses or halls, and which were then bought by the local Hindu community and converted. Even when a Hindu temple in Britain is purpose-built it tends to look different from most temples in India. One reason for this is that in Britain the temple is often part of a bigger building which will serve various other purposes. It will probably be used as a community centre where classes can be held, weddings can be celebrated and meals can be served. For many Hindus, however, the main place of regular worship is in the home rather than in the temple. At regular times, Mina's home serves as a temple when friends come to worship there.

So far, no temple built in Britain has the complex decoration and design of some of the famous Indian temples. Nor will you find along a British road the very simple shrines that abound in India (like the one on p 5) where a tree or a stone may be worshipped by passers-by as an image of God. Given the Hindu belief that God is present in all people and all physical matter, it is not difficult to understand how natural objects, such as stones and rivers, and living things, such as trees and animals, can be a focus for worship.

1 If there is a Hindu temple not far from your school, your teacher may be able to arrange a visit. If you live too far away from a temple ask your teacher to show you a video or slides of a Hindu temple. Information on visiting a temple and on videos and slides is in *Approaches to Hinduism* by Robert Jackson and Dermot Killingley (John Murray, 1988).

Two massive towers which form part of a huge, ancient temple in Tirukalikundram, south India. You can see images of the gods carved on the outside. Old temples in India often have a pool of water in which people can bathe before going inside to pray. The building itself is not just a large hall. It may have many pillars, carved with human and animal figures. The holiest part of the temple may be a small, dark shrine containing the image of the god or goddess. Only the priests can enter this shrine.

Symbols and Images

Fire

'When a person gets married we have fire, and when that person dies he or she is cremated. So fire is there throughout our lives.' This remark was made by a worshipper during the festival of Holi, which features a bonfire. It shows the importance of fire in the Hindu tradition. Throughout history, and all over the world, people have worshipped fire as God or seen it as a symbol of God's power. Without its warmth we cannot live but there is a dangerous side to its power, too.

In Sanskrit, an ancient Indian language which is still used for prayers, the word for fire is 'agni' and this is the name Hindus give to the god of fire. During ceremonies to mark important occasions many Hindus light a fire in a special metal container as part of worship. The flames are fed with sweet smelling herbs and ghi. Ghi is made by boiling butter so that it becomes very pure. People sit crosslegged near the fire and repeat ancient prayers. This type of worship is called 'havan' or 'yagna' and dates back to the time of the Vedas, the oldest Hindu scriptures. In the picture you can see a havan taking place in the Anands' home on a special occasion, but every day in their homes and temples Hindus light little lamps as a way of welcoming God's presence. Some are tiny clay saucers with a wick made from twisted cotton wool. This sort of lamp is called a diva. An arti lamp is usually larger. On p 30 Mina described how an arti lamp is used, and on p 27 there is a picture of one.

Above right: **When a Hindu couple get married the most important part of the wedding takes place around the fire. It reminds everyone that God is witnessing the marriage.**

Left: **For an important occasion the Anand family have a havan in their home. In this case they are about to take part in the mundan ceremony, which marks the occasion when a boy's hair is cut for the first time.**

Weddings

In the picture the couple wearing garlands of flowers and seated behind the fire are the bride and groom at a Hindu wedding, held at a community centre in an English town. The marriage ceremony is a long one but the most important point is when the bride and groom walk around the sacred fire in a clockwise direction. Usually this is done four or seven times and it marks the point at which the couple become husband and wife. This is one Hindu woman's explanation of the four circlings of the fire.

❨During the first three rounds the groom is in the front, the wife following, signifying 'I shall follow you wherever you go – in happiness or in hard times'. On the final round, the bride goes in front and the groom follows. This signifies that during old age, when the time for departing comes, the woman makes her wishes... to die first and not be left behind as a widow.❩

1 It is not only religious people who express deep ideas through symbols. At times of great sadness or joy, symbols and symbolic action are needed to express such feelings. Write a paragraph about any examples you can think of.

2 With a group of friends, write down two reasons why you think people use fire as a symbol for God. Put your ideas into a poster, painting or crayon drawing.

The Lotus

Another 'natural' symbol with meaning to Hindus is the lotus, a kind of water lily. You can often see it in pictures of gods and goddesses. There is a painting of an open lotus flower beneath the statues of Krishna and Radha at the temple in Wellingborough visited by Mina (p 11).

Although its roots are based in thick mud, the lotus opens out into a beautiful flower. It reminds Hindus that though they live in the world, they should, like the lotus, be pure. As Mina says, 'No matter where you are, you can always be the lotus in the mud.'

Swastika and Om

Some Hindus say that fire is the best symbol for God. They argue that if pictures of gods and goddesses are used as symbols, people may think that these really are God. Most Hindus, however, prefer to have a picture in front of them when they worship. There are other kinds of Hindu signs and symbols, however. One of these is the swastika.

Swastika is a Sanskrit word meaning 'bringing health'. It is used as a sign of God's blessing whenever anyone begins something new. When Hindus offer a coconut in puja they usually mark it first with a red swastika. Often a swastika is painted on the doorway of a house or on the first page of an account book. The same shape – a cross with arms of equal length and a line at right angles to each arm of the cross – has been popular with people of many religions, including Christianity, and in many parts of the world. You see it worked into patterns on the pottery of ancient Greece.

Sadly, the swastika has been used in an evil way this century but it had nothing to do with Hinduism. The Nazis, Hitler's nationalist party in Germany, chose a form of swastika as their emblem. They were responsible for the deaths of millions of Jews and others, and forced Europe into a devastating World War.

1 The swastika is a symbol that has changed in meaning and for different groups can mean different things. Here are some other symbols that have had different meanings at various times or to different groups of people: the union flag ('Union Jack'); the star of David; the crucifix. With a group of friends, ask some relatives or teachers about the ideas they associate with these symbols. Share your findings with the rest of the class.

2 Design your own symbol to represent (**a**) energy or (**b**) gentleness.

The picture in this shrine to Shiva in a Coventry Hindu Temple is draped with a cloth bearing a swastika symbol.

In the picture you can see a sign rather like a number three. You may have noticed it earlier in this book in the picture of Meera (p 25). This is actually a syllable – om or aum – in the Sanskrit language. Its sound rhymes with 'dome'. It is impossible to translate 'om' into one English word because for Hindus it is so full of meaning. This is how Mina describes it: 'Om was the first sound. From it came all the rest of creation.' She explains that it really consists of three sounds – A, U, M. Each of these represents a different aspect of God: as creator, destroyer and sustainer. Like many Hindus, Mina repeats this word before praying. She says it slowly so that the sound seems to echo deep within her body and all around her. When a family organises a special act of worship, they may make the sign of om for the occasion, out of red powder or using coloured desiccated coconut on a round metal thali (tray). Some people paint it in red on the doorstep. The om sign is also sometimes put up in the crematorium chapel for a Hindu funeral.

3 Look back at the picture of Princess Meera on p 25. What do you think is the meaning of 'om' in the picture? Look at the shaft of light going from Krishna's hand to the golden bowl for a clue.

'Om', made with rice and seven different sorts of lentils sprinkled with glitter. This was prepared by someone for a special ceremony marking the end of a fast.

In this picture you can see two of Mrs Soni's nieces, who live in Coventry. Each one is carrying on her head a brass waterpot. These have been wrapped in decorated cloths as a sign of respect for the holy water which they contain. One holds Ganga jal (water from the river Ganges). The other contains water from the river Yamuna, a tributary of the Ganga. Both pots had been sealed in India with a metal lid.

Everyone is excited because the pots brought by Mrs Soni all the way from India, will be opened today. The women have been singing, dancing and throwing grains of rice, petals and nuts over the waterpots. In their excitement they have streaked the girl's cheeks with red powder as well as marking their foreheads. Red is a colour of happiness and celebration in India.

Water

Water, like fire, is a natural symbol. It is one of the most important elements of life, for we cannot survive without it. As well as life, water represents purity. In the Hindu tradition its power to cleanse and refresh reminds worshippers that not only must their clothes and body be clean, but also their thoughts should be pure.

Water is often used during acts of Hindu worship. You can see an example of this on p 34. Often the liquid used in puja is not ordinary tap water, but contains water from one of India's holy rivers. Water – especially that from holy rivers – also reminds worshippers of the presence of God. On p 16 you can read the story of how Ganga came to earth. That story helps Hindus to understand the special place of the river and of the goddess Ganga in their religious tradition.

Hindus value highly the rivers of India. They like to visit holy places beside the Ganga, Yamuna and other rivers and to return home with small pots of the sacred water. The opening of one of these pots is a happy occasion, sometimes celebrated with friends and family. On p 27 you can see Mrs Soni at her home in Bombay. She often comes to England to visit her family. On one visit to her sister's house in Coventry a special celebration called a loti utsav was held. An utsav is a celebration and a loti is a small waterpot. The pictures on these pages illustrate the loti utsav.

There are often more women than men at Hindu religious ceremonies. This is not only because more men are out at work. Women have always played an important part in keeping Hindu tradition alive. They enjoy attending celebrations like this which are opportunities for meeting their friends, singing and sharing God's blessing.

The pots were placed in the shrine near the pictures of gods and goddesses. Mrs Soni took a hammer and a long nail and made two holes in the metal lid which had sealed each pot. Now some of the precious water could be poured into two small stainless steel bowls so that everyone could have a sip of Ganga and Yamuna water.

This illustration shows Mrs Soni offering a woman a spoonful of water while another waits, her hands cupped ready to receive the water. One after another, the women received the water, drank it and wiped any remaining drops on their hair. In this way none was wasted and they felt they had been blessed by the holy water.

1 Religions involve the performance of actions which have a meaning. Sometimes the actions are accompanied by words that are spoken or sung. These actions are called rituals. Water is often used in religious rituals. Find out about the use of water in Christian rituals such as baptism. Make a list showing some similarities and differences between the meaning of rituals using water in Christianity and Hinduism. Explain your list to a friend.

This woman is drinking a few drops of holy water during the arti ceremony at a Hindu temple in Coventry. Incense sticks were lit to purify the room and fire, water and food were offered to the gods. After the arti hymn was sung, the lamp was taken round the congregation and then everyone was offered a few drops of water and a little food (fruit or sweets). In the picture a woman drinks some water that has been poured into her right hand from a small brass ladle. This act of worship reminds her of the presence of God and leaves her feeling she has been blessed and purified.

The Shiva linga

Shiva, like Krishna, is shown in many ways. He is often shown dancing, as a way of reminding us that every particle of our universe is moving all the time. Sometimes he is shown with a snake around his neck and with the Ganga flowing from his hair as a reminder of the story told on p 16. Often Hindus pray in front of a linga, which is another way of representing Shiva. The words 'linga' and 'lingam' mean 'sign' in Sanskrit. The linga looks like a short pillar, rounded at the top. In origin the linga is probably a male fertility symbol, showing that Shiva is connected with creation as well as with destruction.

Sometimes, for a particular act of worship, a temporary linga is made out of the clay from a river. Others are made from wood, metal, stone and even from precious gems. Sculptors have to follow exact rules which state how wide the linga must be if it is a certain height. Hindus feel that lingas in certain places are particularly special because they were made by nature, not by the human hand. One of the most famous is high in the mountains at Amarnath. It is an icicle, deep in a sacred cave. Another is a black stone linga in a temple by the sea at Somnath, in the state of Gujarat.

This shrine to Shiva is at the Sannyas Ashram temple in Bombay. The centrepiece is a black Shiva linga. What symbols can you see painted in white on the linga? Which of these are specially connected with Shiva?

Behind the Shiva linga is an image of Shiva's wife, the goddess Parvati. There are two pictures of Shiva (one is on a calendar) in the form of a holy man. You can also see a statue of a coiled cobra, another symbol of Shiva. The priest attends the shrine and performs puja there. Worshippers come to make offerings of flowers or money and to get a glimpse or 'darshan' of Shiva's image.

The linga at Somnath. You can see that flowers, leaves and a coconut have been offered by worshippers. Water drips on to the linga from the container which hangs over it. On the left, facing the linga, is a marble statue of Nandi, Shiva's bull.

Listening to Hindus in this book, it is clear that their religion is full of variety. People worship different gods and goddesses, seeing particular ones as more important to them personally at certain times. The gods Brahma, Vishnu and Shiva are often thought of as the three main aspects of God. As Brahma, God creates the world, as Vishnu he keeps it going, as Shiva he destroys it. If you look at the world around you, especially the world of nature, you will see that this cycle of beginning, reaching maturity and dying is happening all the time.

In south India, Shiva is often shown emerging from a fiery linga. Hindus who worship Shiva tell the story behind this image.

The pillar of fire

The gods Vishnu and Brahma were arguing, each one claiming to be the most important god. As they argued, Shiva appeared as a huge blazing pillar which seemed to have no beginning or end. Brahma turned into a goose so that he could fly up high to find the top of the pillar. Vishnu decided to find out how far down the base of the pillar was. He turned into a boar and dived down. Neither Vishnu nor Brahma could find the ends of the pillar and so eventually they agreed that neither of them was the greatest god. Shiva, they decided, had proved that he was the greatest of all.

1 With a group of friends, discuss why you think this story came to be told. Share your ideas with the rest of the class.

2 Many pictures in Hindu homes and temples tell a story or an incident from a story. Draw or paint a picture that illustrates the story of Shiva as a pillar of fire.

Left: Krishna is often depicted playing a flute and wearing a peacock feather. He can be also recognised by his bluish colour. One story tells that a wicked demon wanted to kill young children. She turned herself into a beautiful young mother who went around offering her breast milk to small children in the villages. The milk was poisoned and the children who drank it died. When she went to baby Krishna's village, he drank the milk. But, because he was God in human form, Krishna survived and the wicked demon disintegrated into ashes. The poison gave Krishna a blue appearance but did not harm him. In this picture you can see him with his beautiful companion Radha. You can read more about Krishna on p 22.

Right: Jalaram Bapa. Thousands of people visit the place in Virpur where Jalaram lived. Here they eat a free meal, remembering how he never refused to give food to those visited him.

Religious pictures

Many Hindus find it easier to express their love for God if they have pictures of some of the different forms of God to look at. To outsiders it may seem as if there are lots of gods but to many Hindus these are just different glimpses of the one God, who is too great for human beings to imagine. Members of a family may not all choose to pray to the same god or goddess. Nowadays there are a lot of Indian films showing the Hindu gods and

paintings and designs done in India. Hindu children are used to seeing religious pictures in their homes, and not only in the room where they worship. To advertise their shop, Hindu shopkeepers in India and elsewhere often give their customers calendars with pictures of gods, goddesses or saints. These pictures allow worshippers to have a glimpse (darshan) of the god or goddess, who is usually portrayed looking out from the print, directly at the viewer.

Hindus often display photographs of people whom they respect, for example, their guru and their parents if they have died. Around the picture, they hang garlands made from flowers or twisted shavings of sweet-smelling sandalwood.

goddesses. Sometimes a whole film is about one of them, such as Santoshi Ma. People recognise the gods and goddesses because they are used to seeing their statues and pictures and there are always certain clues to their identity. For instance Saraswati, the goddess of learning, is accompanied by a swan or a peacock. She has a stringed musical instrument with her called a vina. Some gods are shown as part animal, part human. Ganesha is easy to recognise as he has the head of an elephant.

Hindu families in Britain, like Mina's family and the Anands, often buy pictures of gods and saints. Some of these are printed in India and are exported to other countries. Some of them are printed in Britain, often from original

Jalaram Bapa

Some people have pictures of saints whom they worship. In many Gujarati homes, for example, there are pictures of Jalaram Bapa. He was a merchant who lived in Virpur, Gujarat, from 1799–1881 and always helped people in need. In the picture you can see him holding his mala and his stick. It is believed that Lord Rama came to his house disguised as an aged traveller who needed someone to look after him on his journey. Jalaram Bapa sent his wife to assist him, even though it was unusual for a man to send his wife off with a stranger. By doing this Jalaram Bapa showed that he had complete trust in God. When they reached a river, the old man handed Jalaram Bapa's stick back to her and disappeared. At the same time, Jalaram Bapa heard a voice saying that the old man was Lord Rama, who had come to test his goodness and faith.

1 Make a list of the different kinds of pictures you have displayed in your room at home and why you chose them. Write down some reasons why you like to have pictures to look at. Share your ideas with the rest of the class.

Images

Hindus believe that prayers can be said anywhere and at any time, but most Hindus like to visit a temple sometimes, to make offerings in front of statues or images of gods and goddesses. The images in a temple are treated with great respect – the same respect that would be given to an honoured guest, or even to a king or queen. It is the priest's duty to make sure that food is offered daily and that the image is washed and dressed. The image is not always on show to give people darshan – a glimpse or sight of the statue which gives the worshipper God's blessing. The curtains are drawn across when the food has been offered. Images are often made of stone and they are carved according to strict traditional rules about the exact proportions for temple sculptures. No statue can be used in worship if it is damaged or imperfect.

In the picture you can see a diagram on a blackboard explaining the correct proportions of an image of a god. The diagram was drawn for students studying for a diploma at a college of sculpture in Mahabalipuram, in the state of Tamil Nadu in south India. By learning this information about images and the skills to carve them, young sculptors keep alive a tradition that goes back for many centuries. The college is only a short distance from the huge rock carving of the descent of the Ganga which is over a thousand years old (pp 16–17).

In Britain, temple committees place an order for a statue with craftsmen in India and pay for the finished image to be transported by air to this country. In 1988 some new marble images were installed at a temple in Coventry. They had been carved specially for the temple by craftsmen in Jaipur, in the state of Rajasthan in north India. You can imagine the excitement when they finally arrived in Coventry after their long journey. In the picture you can see the lorry which carried the images, or murtis, through the local streets. In this way Hindus feel that gods and goddesses give their blessing to the onlookers and to the

Left: A college in Mahabalipuram in south India where young men learn the traditional ways to make images. The diagram on the blackboard shows the correct proportions for an image. The writing on the right-hand blackboard is in the ancient language of Sanskrit. It is a hymn to the weather god, Indra.

Right: The lorry in this picture is at the head of a procession through Coventry. It is carrying new images which have been made in India and paid for by Hindus who wish to install them in a temple in Coventry.

neighbourhood.

There are disagreements between followers of different religions, and even within religions, about the use of images as a focus for worship. Those people who argue against the use of images usually say that worshippers will tend to worship the image itself and not God whom the image represents. But many worshippers find it very helpful to have an image or picture on which to concentrate during worship.

It is easy to see why images are popular in Hinduism. Since many Hindus believe God to be present everywhere and in everything, God must be present in images as well as in people and other things. Also, images or pictures often remind worshippers of stories that have a spiritual or moral point to them, such as the story of Jagannath which is recalled by seeing his image (p 19). Some of them are like a 'freeze frame' of a film: one image which sums up the whole meaning of the story. The pictures of Santoshi Ma (p 32), Shiva (p 17) and the baby

Krishna (p 22) are good examples of this. Even so, there are disagreements about images within the Hindu tradition. For many Hindus, the spirit of God is especially present in an image after the ceremony at which it is first installed in a temple. For others, images are no more than a focus or an aid to help them concentrate on their devotions. For a few, such as members of a Hindu sect called the Arya Samaj, images should not be used at all since, it is argued, they were not used in ancient times when the Vedas, the oldest texts of Hinduism, were first used.

---

1 With a group of friends, think of reasons why some religious people find pictures and images of gods or saints helpful in worship and why others believe it is wrong to use them. Share your ideas with the rest of the class.

Installing an image

The day when the new images were installed was an important one for people who attend the Hindu Mandir in Coventry. Most of the people who go to the temple, like the Anands, have a family history that goes back to the state of Punjab in north-west India, but on this special day Hindus from other communities were also present. The President of the National Council of Hindu Temples was there and Babu Govind Garala was present as secretary of the Shree Krishna Mandir, another Coventry temple. There were other important guests, including the Lord Mayor of Coventry who spoke about the contribution that the Hindu communities have made to the life of the city. Subhash Anand, as secretary of the Hindu Mandir, was helping to organise the

event and making sure that everything happened on time.

The heavy statues, including the one of the goddess Mataji you can see in the picture, were carried carefully into the temple. Prayers and hymns had been sung already for two days before this ceremony. Grains of wheat and rice had been offered in front of the images. Rice and wheat are symbols of life

The statue of Mataji, which has just been installed in the temple. Looking at her are members of the family who donated the statue. In her hands the goddess holds symbols of her power. With the weapons she destroys evil, but she also blesses and rewards people who are good.

because we depend on food which is made from them. From this point on, the worshippers felt that God was especially present in the images.

As well as the installation ceremony, the celebrations included music and a play put on by some of the children who go to the temple. Ashish Anand played the dholki and the tabla, different types of drum, and his sisters, Saral and Sheetal, took part in the drama. Saral played the part of Krishna and was dressed like him during his time as a young cowherd. She used her school recorder as Krishna's flute.

Many temples have at least one image of the goddess (Devi). Hindus have various names for her, including Mataji, Ambaji and Ambe Mata. Mata means 'mother' and 'ji' makes the name more respectful. When she is shown riding on a tiger, Punjabis often call her Sheranwali Mata, which, in Punjabi, means, 'the mother on the tiger'.

Statues like those installed at the temple will last for hundreds of years but for some festivals temporary images are made by craftsmen. For instance, in Bengal, clay images of the goddess Durga are immersed in the river after the festival of Durga Puja is over.

---

1 Give reasons why you think Hindus wash their image of God and offer food to it. It may help you if you think of ways in which you would treat an important visitor to your home.

2 Look carefully at the pictures in this chapter. Write down in your own words or draw as a poster some of the different ways in which Hindus represent God.

Special Occasions

Amit's mundan

Birthdays come every year but some special occasions occur only once in a lifetime. For Hindus, several of these take place when Hindu children are almost too young to remember what happens. One ceremony for small boys is the mundan, when the boy's hair is all shaved off. Until this moment, it has been allowed to grow without being cut at all. Sometimes it gets quite long and is tied back. Different families have different customs. As the Anands are Punjabi, their customs and festivals are those followed by people from Punjab. Many Hindus say that the mundan must happen in the year before their son's first birthday or in the year before his third or fifth birthday. Sometimes a boy's family may be planning to have the mundan but then have to postpone it for over a year. This happens if a member of the family dies, because no celebration can take place until a full year has passed after the death.

The mundan ceremony for Subhash Anand's son, Amit, took place the day before his third birthday. Subhash explains its importance to the family.

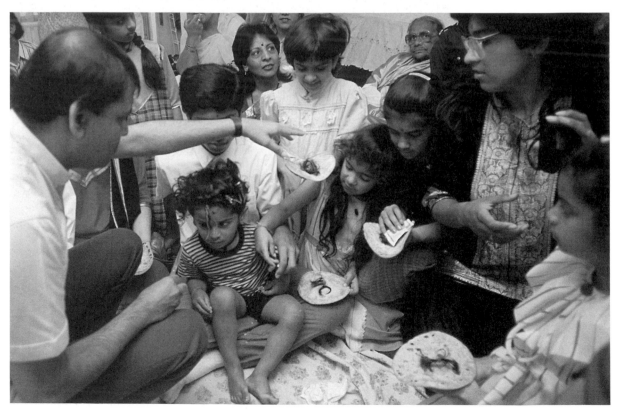

❝The mundan ceremony is part of our Hindu ritual activities which we perform during the life span. When the child is born the first ritual we do is the nām samskār – we give the child its real name. The second ceremony is the mundan – the shaving of the head. The hair isn't cut at all until the day of the mundan.❞

People like to follow the customs of their community. They feel happier in their own mind if these have taken place, especially when young children are involved. It is also an opportunity for relations to gather together.

Centuries ago people probably shaved their young children's heads because they thought they would be cleaner and healthier. Sometimes Hindus say that by removing the hair which a baby had even before it was born, they are removing traces of its previous life. By carrying out religious rituals like the mundan, people express their wish to keep their children safe from harm.

Right: Amit sits in his brother's lap as the barber shaves off the rest of his hair. The hair will be wrapped in a cloth and put in a river. The chapatis can be offered to the birds.

Left: Amit's sisters and cousin-sisters tied locks of his long hair with strands of wool. You can see that the barber has cut these locks first and put them on chapatis which were specially made for the mundan. Doing this is a way of wishing Amit a happy, healthy life. This is because chapatis are made from wheat, which is a symbol for life.

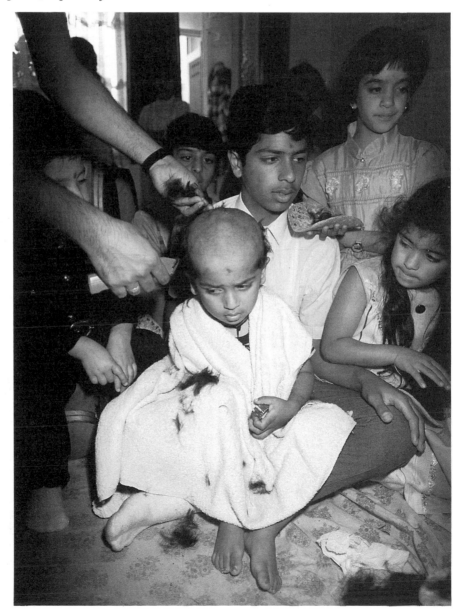

After the barber had shaved off all Amit's hair he was given a bath. First he was smeared with cool, creamy yoghurt, because it is made from milk which, like the cow, is respected as holy. Then he was given a bath in water. Because it was a hot day, Amit had his bath in the paddling pool in the garden! He was dressed in smart new clothes and a white turban was put on his head. On top of this, as you see in the photograph below, he wore a turban-shaped hat. Amit's uncle (his mother's brother) paid for these special clothes. Even if a boy's uncle lives too far away to be present he will be and will feel involved in the mundan ceremony in some way.

Both men and women sometimes have their heads shaved when they are grown up, as a sign that they will from now on follow the teachings of a particular guru. There are also some temples in India where people go when they have made a special promise in the name of the god or goddess who is worshipped there. When they arrive, they have their heads shaved to show that they have kept their vow.

1 If you have never come across a mundan ceremony before you might find some parts of it a little unusual: the head shaving and the bathing with yoghurt, for example. Choose one of the following situations or events and pretend that you are a visitor from another culture who has never witnessed it before and finds it rather strange: a wedding in a church (including what happens outside after the ceremony); a game of rugby or American football; a birthday party. Write down a list of questions you would need to ask in order to understand the situation or event.

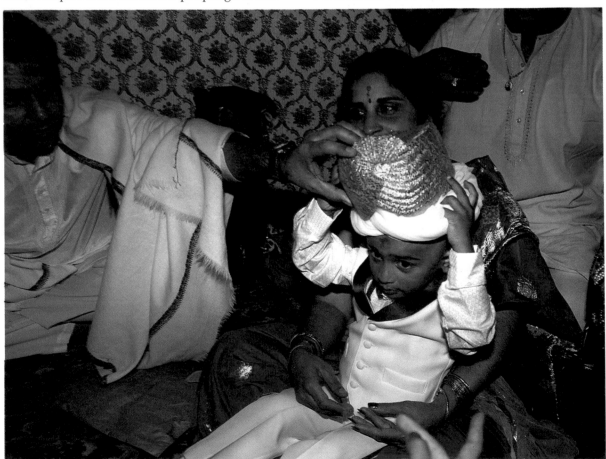

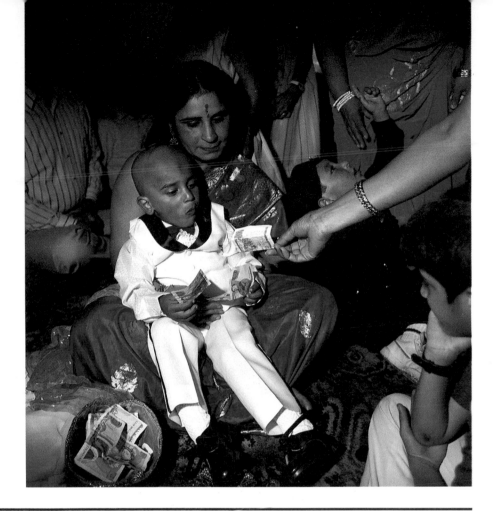

Amit sits on Mrs Anand's knee as he receives £5 notes from the relations and friends who came to see his mundan.

2 With a group of friends make a short tape-recorded feature for a children's radio programme in which you describe and explain Amit's mundan. There's no need to write everything down. Plan what each person is going to say and then record it section by section. If you are not happy with what you have said, you can erase it and do another 'take'. Play your feature to the rest of the class.

3 Can you think of any times when you have taken part in or been at a ceremony which shows that a person is starting a new stage of their life? Baptism (or christening), confirmation, enrolment into Scouts or Guides and a wedding are just some possibilities. Write down any three things you can remember from one of these occasions in which you've taken part. Share your memories and comments with other members of your class.

4 Bring to school any objects you have that symbolise the beginning of a new stage of life. Examples might be a baptism certificate; your Cub or Scout cap or Brownie hat; photographs of you or members of your family at an event such as a christening, wedding, or when moving house or starting a school. Your class could mount an exhibition or prepare a class assembly on 'Beginnings'.

5 Find out about 'joining' or initiation ceremonies in one other religion. Some examples are baptism and confirmation (Christianity); bar mitzvah and bat mitzvah (Judaism) and the amrit ceremony (Sikhism). Make a list of some similarities to and differences from Amit's mundan ceremony, taking care to think about
(a) the rituals and
(b) their meaning.

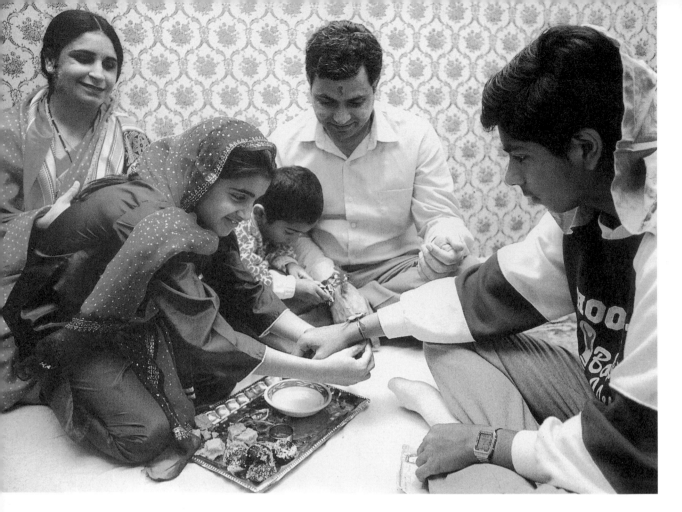

Raksha Bandhan

During the year Hindu children in Britain look forward to their birthdays and to Christmas – when they too decorate the house and celebrate with their relatives. Christmas is not a Hindu festival but Hindu families in Britain do not want their children to miss out on the fun. They like going to parties and giving and receiving presents. There are other days to look forward to as well. Hindus have many festivals which they enjoy celebrating each year. But if a relative died on a festival day their family would no longer celebrate it. In this way they remember their relation.

Diwali is a particularly favourite festival. Hindu homes and temples are bright with candles and in the evening children let off fireworks. There are many stories connected with Diwali. One tells how Rama and Sita had

While their mother and a friend watch, Saral ties a rakhi on her brother Ashish's right wrist. Because it is a religious act, both have covered their heads. You can also see the bowl of plain yoghurt which some people put out for the ceremony. Yoghurt is often used on special occasions, because anything connected with cows and milk is holy.

to spend fourteen years in exile. During this time Ravana, a demon king, carried Sita off to Sri Lanka. With the help of an army of animals Rama rescued her and they returned to his kingdom where people let off fireworks because they were so happy. Lakshmi, the goddess of prosperity, is worshipped at this time as well. People clean their houses and

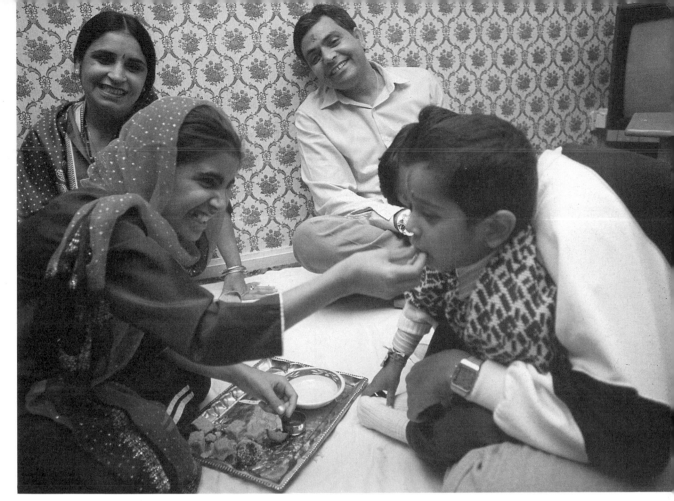

paint patterns, hoping Lakshmi will visit their home and bless it with wealth. Sometimes they act out the story of King Rama and Queen Sita.

Another favourite festival day is Raksha Bandhan which is often called Rakhi. This usually takes place in the month of August. It is always celebrated on the day before the full moon in Shravan. Hindus have a special calendar which follows the moon and Shravan is the name for one of the twelve lunar months.

Adults as well as children celebrate the Raksha Bandhan festival. It is a time for sisters and brothers to show their affection. In the morning, before eating anything, girls tie a colourful thread, often with a round shiny decoration on it, on their brother's right wrist. This thread is called a rakhi.

For Saral Anand, Raksha Bandhan is one of the best festivals of the year. It is a way of showing how much she cares for her brother.

After tying the rakhi on her brothers' wrists and marking their foreheads with a dab of red powder, Saral gives them large Indian sweets. Ashish holds Amit, while their sister Saral puts a laddu (an Indian sweet) in his mouth.

❲Sisters tie a special string called a rakhi on the brother's hand to show their love for him. If the brother is working and he looks at his wrist, he'll remember his sister because he's got that rakhi on it. And I must put a tika – a small round dot – on his forehead. My Mum will do the same to her brother.❳

Raksha Bandhan is a festival when brothers also show their love for their sisters. All through his life a brother is expected to help his sister whenever she might need it. Brothers give their sisters gifts, usually money, and later on they may give presents to their sisters' children on important occasions, as Amit's uncle did for the mundan ceremony (see p 50). Hindus feel that cousins are also their brothers and sisters. They often call them 'brother' or 'sister' or use the words 'cousin-brother' and 'cousin-sister'. If a sister or cousin-sister lives somewhere else, she sends the rakhi by post. Ashish explains.

❝I will also give presents of money or some other kind of gift to my sisters, and to my

56

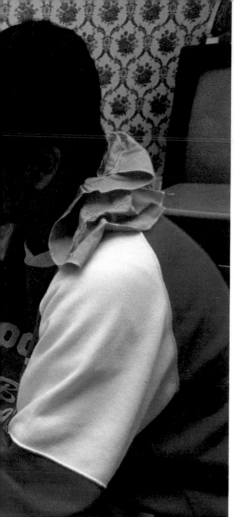

cousin-sisters as well. My relationship with them should be the same as between me and my sisters. We often send sugar as a sweet. I get sent rakhis from cousins in India. My sister Saral will tie them on for me but it will be *their* faces that I'll see when she ties it on to my wrist.*"*

There is a story that many years ago a king was going to invade a queen's territory. Fortunately, she got to hear of his plans. It was the time of Raksha Bandhan, so she sent him a rakhi. This meant that he had to behave like a brother and protect her. He could not attack her as an enemy any more, and so she and her kingdom were saved from invasion.

Left: Ashish gives £5 notes to his sisters, Saral and Sheetal.

Below: Saral and Sheetal have tied rakhis on Ashish's right wrist.

Bhumi puja

In 1987 Hindus in Coventry bought a plot of land on which they hoped to have a purpose-built temple. Hundreds of people came to a special ceremony called bhumi puja or worship of the earth. Gujarati girls walked to the plot of land in a procession. Each girl had a round pot of holy water on her head. In the water there were drops of Ganga water. The girls said their arms ached afterwards, from trying to hold the pot in place! After the procession the bhumi puja ceremony was held in a marquee, where a havan, or offering of fire, was taking place. Babu Govind Garala explains bhumi puja.

❛The religious importance of the bhumi puja ceremony is that it purifies the ground that we humans have made impure over the centuries, so that we can build a new temple on the site. To the best of my knowledge this has not happened in Britain before. Personally, I think the ceremony marks a turning point for Hindus in Britain. We had a sannyasi, a holy man from India, called Swami Satyamitranand Giri, who took part in the ceremony and also gave a lecture on the importance of bhumi puja. Such holy men ensure that our communities are in touch with the ancient traditions of India.❜

1 Find out what the term 'consecrated ground' means to members of some Christian churches, such as the Church of England, and for what purposes consecrated ground may and may not be used.

Left: On special occasions Gujarati Hindu girls carry a coconut and a pot of holy water on their heads. This picture shows a procession from an old temple in Coventry to the site where a new one is to be specially built.

Right: As the procession reaches the site of the new temple, each girl is welcomed and a special red tika mark is put on her forehead.

श्री गणेशाय नमः

श्रीकृष्ण - मंदिर

શ્રી હિંદુ સત્સંગ મંડળ કોવેન્ટ્રી.

શ્રી ખાત-મુહુર્ત અને શ્રી શીલારોપણ મહોત્સવ

જાહેર આમંત્રણ

SHREE KRISHNA MANDIR
Shree Hindu Satsang Mandal, Coventry

92 A Stoney Stanton Road,
Coventry CV1 4FL
Tel: (0203) 23633

Laying the foundation stone

Some months after the bhumi puja, a further special event took place at the site of the new temple. The foundation stone was laid, fulfilling a longstanding wish of the Garala family. Babu Govind Garala explains:

❝The laying of the foundation stone was important to the Gujarati Hindu community because it was the first stone of our new temple and community centre. It was especially important to me because it was the

60

wish of my late father, Govind Garala, that we should have a purpose-built temple in this city. Our family was involved in performing the religious ceremony and laying the stone in memory of my late father. Some people had lost hope that we would ever have a purpose-built temple in Coventry, so the ceremony gave people faith that it would be built.**)**

Laying the foundation stone was part of a bigger ceremony. A procession came from the old temple and there was a havan in a tent on

the building site. A trench was excavated for the stone. The surveyor and architect were there, as it had to be laid exactly under the centre point of the future temple and community centre.

The stone was a large block of marble inscribed with symbols. These included a tortoise, a conch shell and water. These symbols have different meanings and remind people of the ancient stories in which they play a part. Vishnu was born as a tortoise before being born in the forms of Rama and Krishna. A famous story tells how when the gods and demons were fighting they churned the ocean round and round, in the same way as butter is still churned in villages in India. In the story, the churning stick was kept steady on the shell of the tortoise – tortoises can keep perfectly still for a very long time – and its back provided a firm base. The conch shell is blown like a trumpet when Hindus are worshipping God. It represents all and every kind of sound. You can see one in the picture of Ganesha on p 7. In this book you have already heard about ways in which water is used in worship and believed to be special.

You can imagine the suspense as the heavy piece of marble was lowered to exactly the right spot. A prayer was said and flowers were put on the stone. Then it was completely covered with liquid concrete. A few months later the building of the new temple began.

---

1 With a group of friends think of any similarity between Amit's mundan ceremony (p 50) and the laying of the foundation stone. Share your ideas with the rest of the class.

2 The Indian language on the invitation card is Gujarati. In Gujarati 'Shree' is a title which shows respect. This word appears 5 times on the card. Can you work out which one it is and copy it onto a piece of paper? 'Coventry' and 'Shree' end with the same letter in Gujarati. Which is the Gujarati word for Coventry? Copy out the second line of Gujarati. This says Shree Krishna Mandir, the name of the temple.

The new Shree Krishna temple as it was in July 1989 when the main body of the building was complete. In 1989 the new temple won a national prize (the Community Enterprise Award) which was presented to members of the temple by Prince Charles at a ceremony in London.

Index and Glossary

Most of these words and names come from the Indian languages of Sanskrit and Hindi. These languages have an alphabet with more letters than the English alphabet. There are several ways of writing Indian words in English, so you may see some of them spelt differently in other books. For instance 'Diwali' could be spelt 'Divali', and 'Meera' could be written as 'Mira'.

This is a guide to the pronunciation of these words and names. A vowel with a line above it indicates a different pronunciation from the same vowel without a line. The vowels are pronounced as follows: 'a' is pronounced like the 'a' in 'human', and 'ā' like 'a' in 'far; 'i' is pronounced like 'i' in 'fit' and 'ī' like 'ee' in 'feet'; 'u' is pronounced like 'u' in 'pull' and 'ū' like 'oo' in 'moon'.

Ārtī 13, 30, 34, 36   worshipping God by moving a small oil light reverently in front of a religious picture or statue

Bhagavād Gītā 12, 15, 23   a holy book containing Krishna's teachings

Bhajan 24, 30   hymn

Brahma 7, 16, 17, 43   one of the three principal forms of God

Brāhmin 28, 29   member of the castes to which priests belong

Caste 28   the word for a large group of families whose ancestors had the same occupation

Conch 13, 61   a large white shell which can be blown like a trumpet

Darshan 30, 42, 45, 46   a 'glimpse', receiving a blessing by being in the presence of a god, goddess or holy person

Dēvī 33, 49   goddess

Dīvā 36   a small lamp, usually a tiny clay bowl in which a wick, made from cotton wool and soaked in oil or ghi, is lit

Diwālī 33   late autumn festival of lights

Durgā 33, 49   a goddess

Ganesha 7, 28, 33, 45, 61   (pronounced Ganesh) elephant-headed god who is believed to remove obstacles

Gangā 8, 17, 28, 46, 59   the Ganges, a river in north India, which is regarded as a goddess

Ghī 31, 36   butter which has been boiled to make it more pure

Goddess 44, 48, 52   God in female form – Hindus do not always imagine God as male

Goynī 33   a girl who plays a special part on some occasions when a goddess is worshipped

Gujarātī 30, 33, 59, 61   this word describes the people and culture of the state of Gujarat on the west coast of India. It is also used for their language and alphabet

Guru 24, 30, 45   a teacher, especially a religious teacher

Holī 36   a spring festival

ISKCON 12, 14   the International Society for Krishna Consciousness, a Hindu organisation also known as the Hare Krishna Movement. Many people who follow the teachings of ISKCON are not Indian

Jagannāth 12, 15, 18, 47   Lord of the Universe, God worshipped in the form of a black image with no arms

Jalarām Bāpā 45   Gujarati saint who lived from 1799 to 1881

Karma 6   the belief that everything we do has an effect on us

Krishna 6, 12, 22, 23, 37, 42, 47, 49, 61   one of the human forms of the god Vishnu

Lakshmī 7, 33, 54   goddess of wealth

Linga 42   a symbol for the god Shiva which looks like a short pillar with a rounded top

Lotus 37   a pink water lily which is used as a religious symbol

Mā, Mātā, Mātājī 33, 48, 49   'mother', titles for the goddess

Meerā 39   a princess who devoted her life to Krishna and composed songs dedicated to him

Mundan 50, 51, 61   head-shaving ceremony

Mūrti 46   statue of a god or goddess

Om 27, 39   a word for God which is often used by Hindus when they pray

Prashād 10, 14, 29, 31, 34   food (often nuts, fruit or Indian sweets) which Hindus share out after an act of worship, believing that the food has been blessed by God because it has been offered at the shrine

Priest 28, 46   a man, usually from a brahmin family, who performs religious ceremonies for Hindu families

Acknowledgements

Our thanks are due to the Hindu communities in Coventry especially to Subhash Anand, Babu Govind Garala, Yashpal Joshi and Ram Krishan and to families who have taken part in the Hindu Nurture in Coventry Project, especially the Anand and Patel families. The project was based in the Arts Education Department at Warwick University and was funded by the Leverhulme Trust whose generous support we gratefully acknowledge. Thanks are also due to Olivia Bennett for her editorial guidance and to Heather Meldrum for her word processing skills and her considerable patience. The quotation from Dr Gokal on p 6 is from *Worlds of Faith* by John Bowker (BBC, 1983). The quotation on p 37 is from *The Hindu Arranged Marriage* by R Patel and N Lambert (YWCA Community Centre, Loughborough).

Robert Jackson and Eleanor Nesbitt

The Publishers would like to thank the following for permission to reproduce photographs.

David Allison 21
Barnabys Picture Library 15
Robert Jackson 5, 7, 8, 9, 10, 16/17, 21, 22, 23, 26, 27, 30, 31, 34, 35, 37, 38, 41, 42, 46, 52, 58, 60, 62
Eleanor Nesbitt 11, 24, 33, 39, 40, 41, 43, 47, 59, 61
David Richardson 48, 49
Liba Taylor 6, 12, 13, 14, 19, 20, 28, 29, 36, 50, 51, 53, 54, 55, 56/57, 57

Cover picture: A brahmin priest conducting a puja with the Anand family at their home (see p 29).